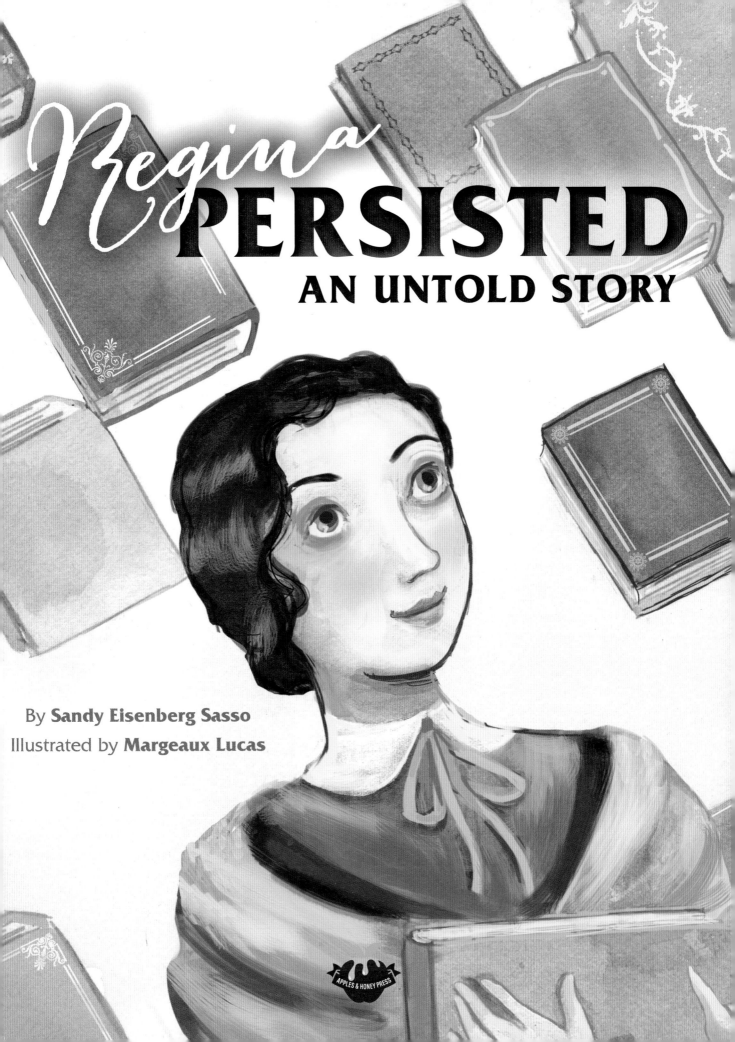

Regina
PERSISTED
AN UNTOLD STORY

By **Sandy Eisenberg Sasso**

Illustrated by **Margeaux Lucas**

APPLES & HONEY PRESS

"I hope a time will come for all of us in which there will be no more questions on the subject of 'women,' for as long as there are questions, something is wrong."
— Regina Jonas

A note from the author: Most of this book is based on biographical material about Regina Jonas. We do not have a record of everything she said or did. So much was lost. So much of her story was never told. This book fills in some of the spaces that history left blank. Special thanks to Professor Katharina von Kellenbach, who found the papers of Regina Jonas, and Rabbi Elisa Klapheck, who wrote her first comprehensive biography.

In memory of my mother, Freda Eisenberg, who never doubted that women could be anything they wanted to be.
— S.E.S

For Sally Lucas, my amazing and wonderful mother, with all my love.
— M.L.

Apples & Honey Press
An imprint of Behrman House
Millburn, New Jersey 07041
www.applesandhoneypress.com

Text copyright © 2018 by Sandy Eisenberg Sasso
Illustrations copyright © 2018 by Margeaux Lucas

ISBN 978-1-68115-540-1

Photograph on page 31 courtesy Stiftung Neue Synagoge Berlin - Centrum Judaicum
Photograph on page 32 by Herbert Warburg, 1939, by permission of Rabbi Amy Joy Small

Library of Congress Cataloging-in-Publication Data

Names: Sasso, Sandy Eisenberg, author. | Lucas, Margeaux, illustrator.
Title: Regina persisted ; an untold story / by Sandy Eisenberg Sasso ;
illustrated by Margeaux Lucas.
Description: Millburn, New Jersey : Apples & Honey Press, [2018]
Identifiers: LCCN 2017033104 | ISBN 9781681155401
Subjects: LCSH: Jonas, Regina, 1902-1944. | Women rabbis--Germany--Juvenile
literature.
Classification: LCC BM755.J72 .S37 2018 | DDC 296.092 [B] --dc23 LC record available at
https://lccn.loc.gov/2017033104

Design by Alexandra N. Segal
Edited by Dena Neusner
Printed in the United States of America
1 3 5 7 9 8 6 4 2

Regina's heart was racing. She knew she needed a good night's rest, but she couldn't sleep. Tomorrow was the last day of her studies, and she was going to take the most important test of all.

If she passed this test, she would become a rabbi.

When the sun rose, Regina was already awake.
She brushed and pinned her thick, dark hair.
She put on her favorite green velvety dress with
the puffy sleeves. Her mother had breakfast
on the table, but Regina couldn't eat.

Regina left for school early. The streets of Berlin
were busy with bicycles, horse-drawn carriages,
and motorcars. Peddlers called out their wares.
The smells of fish, fresh lemon, and
sweet spices filled the air.

"Why so fast today, Regina?" shouted one of the peddlers as she ran past his pushcart overflowing with fruits and vegetables.

"This is one day I am not going to be late," she called back.

Another peddler tossed a fresh roll to Regina. He said, "You know what the rabbis say, 'If there is no bread, there is no Torah.'"

Regina smiled and thanked him as she flew past.

Regina thought about the moments that had led to this day.
As she nibbled on the warm bread, she daydreamed.

She saw herself in her dark, damp apartment, placing her stuffed animals in two rows. Some had little hats on their heads. Regina pretended to read from the Torah and then raised it for all her furry friends to see. While her girlfriends played house, Regina played rabbi.

Most people in 1913 didn't believe that girls should receive a religious education. They thought girls only needed to learn to make Shabbat and prepare a proper kitchen. But Regina's father taught both his son *and* his daughter Torah and Hebrew.

When Regina was twelve years old, her father died. Sadness filled
the house. Regina said the memorial prayers with her
brother and mother at her father's grave.

She made a promise: "I will carry on the traditions of my father.
Maybe I will even become a rabbi." Her mother smiled sadly and said,
"No woman has ever been a rabbi."

"Not yet!" Regina replied. "I will be what I will be."

Saturday mornings, Regina walked with her brother
and mother to synagogue. Regina hardly noticed the
other boys and girls darting in and out of bushes, playing
hide-and-seek. The synagogue, with its big round arches
and beautiful Ark, was her favorite place.
There she felt at home.

Sometimes, after everyone else had left the synagogue,
Regina would stay to study with the rabbi.
"You are a good student. Would you like to learn
more about Judaism?" he asked.
Regina smiled and nodded.

But people complained. "Stop wasting your time studying with the rabbi," they said. "You should learn to cook and sew like the other girls."

Regina heard, but she persisted.

Honk! Neigh! The street sounds interrupted Regina's daydreams.
The drivers of a horse-drawn carriage and a motorcar were yelling,
"Fräulein, stop dreaming! Watch where you are going!"

Regina arrived at school before any of the other students. She loved the scent of old books that filled the halls. She thought about her final essay for the class, in which she had asked, "Can Women Serve as Rabbis?" Her answer was, "YES! Yes, they can!" Her teachers all agreed.

At least that's what Regina thought.
But when she came to take her test, one of the professors stopped her.

"Regina," he said, "I cannot let you take this exam.
Stop trying to be a rabbi. You won't be—not now, not ever."

Regina's voice broke. "There are women doctors, lawyers, and teachers. There will be a woman rabbi. God created man and woman, and the world cannot be held up by men alone."

The rabbi could not look Regina in the eye. "You'll get over this, my dear. With time you will change your mind." He turned and left Regina alone. For a moment Regina could not move. She could barely breathe.

"I will be what I will be," she said to the empty room.

Regina told her teachers, friends, and neighbors that someday she would be a rabbi. They warned,

"Be careful, don't make trouble!"

"Be a teacher like other women!"

"Women are not smart enough!"

"See how Regina dresses! She doesn't look like a rabbi!"

"Do what you are supposed to do— go home and cook!"

Regina persisted.

She was tired of being interrupted when she spoke.
She was tired of being told what she could not do because she
was a woman.

She was tired of people telling her that when she got older,
she would change her mind.

She continued teaching, even without being called "Rabbi."

Often, Regina would arrive at school late.
Out of breath from running, her
dress wrinkled, she would sit on
her desk and take out the sandwich
she had forgotten to eat.

She loved her students, and they loved her. It didn't
matter that she was messy and her clothes old-fashioned.
Regina always looked her students straight in the eyes.

It was as if she could tell what each one was thinking. She taught the girls in her class, "Use your eyes, ears, hands, and mouth, so that you can see, hear, touch, and taste what it is to be a Jew."

Some parents did not see the point of their daughters studying Torah. But Regina persisted. She told them, "There have been lots of strong Jewish women."

Miriam was a prophet and a great leader. She led the women in dance and song after crossing the Sea of Reeds.

"Miriam, Deborah, and Esther were leaders from the Bible, brave and wise. Your daughters can do great things someday, too."

Deborah was a great prophet and a wise judge.

Esther had the courage to speak out against those who wanted to destroy her people.

It was a hard time to be a Jew in Germany. A group called the Nazis had come to power. People were told not to shop in Jewish stores. There were signs saying, "Do not buy from Jews." Many Jews were afraid and decided to leave Germany.

But Regina stayed. "My mother is too old to start a new life in a new country," she said. "My place is here with my people."

Regina kept studying.

One year passed, then two. Regina persisted. She kept teaching. She attracted large crowds of people. Often there was standing room only.

Three years passed, then four. Regina persisted. In dark times, she taught her students to find joy in Jewish holidays and to dance.

Every year Regina applied to take the test to become a rabbi.
Every year she was told no.

Finally, after five years, the rabbis and teachers
of Berlin began to see Regina clearly. . . .

They saw how much she learned.
They saw her gift for teaching.

They saw the way she cared for others.
They saw her love for the Jewish people.

They saw a woman who was already acting like a rabbi.

On December 26, 1935, Regina Jonas was finally allowed to take the test.

She passed.

At long last, she was a rabbi—the very first woman rabbi in the whole world!

"I will be what I will be."

Dear Readers,

I wonder what it feels like to be the very first at something.
Have you ever had a big dream that someone told you was impossible to
achieve, just because of who you are?

I wonder why Regina Jonas did not just give up when people kept telling her
she was wrong. Do you ever feel like giving up when things get hard?
Have you ever persisted in doing something difficult that you thought was
right, even though others told you that you couldn't?

I wonder what you might need to help you persist in following a dream.
I wonder if there is someone you can help to fulfill his or her dream.

— Rabbi Sandy Eisenberg Sasso

Afterword

After Regina passed the test, her struggles were not over. The Jewish Community of Berlin would not hire her or allow her to lead services at a synagogue. Some cautioned her, "Be careful; do not call yourself 'rabbi.'" One synagogue did invite her to give sermons but not on the main pulpit. Still, Regina persisted. Finally, the Jewish Community of Berlin officially hired Rabbi Regina Jonas in 1937. She lectured, taught, and provided pastoral care throughout the community.

Rare photo of Regina Jonas, 1939

Regina Jonas lived during the time of the Nazis' rise to power in Germany. The Nazis hated people who were not like them, especially the Jews. Little by little, the Nazis took away any rights that the Jews had. They closed their businesses and made them wear yellow stars. They forced them into special camps, called concentration camps. Regina was sent to one of those camps, Theresienstadt. There she lived in horrible conditions with her mother and other Jews. She served as a rabbi in Theresienstadt, bringing comfort to others and teaching them to be proud of being Jews. In 1944 she was taken to Auschwitz where she was killed. For more than forty years, no one told her story.

It was not until 1972 that a woman was again ordained as a rabbi. Rabbi Sally Priesand was ordained by the Reform movement's Hebrew Union College-Jewish Institute of Religion, in Cincinnati. Two years later, Rabbi Sandy Eisenberg Sasso was the first woman ordained by the Reconstructionist Rabbinical College in Philadelphia. In 1985, Rabbi Amy Eilberg became the first woman ordained in the Conservative movement by the Jewish Theological Seminary in New York. Rabba Sara Hurwitz was ordained in 2009 by Rabbi Avi Weiss of the Orthodox Hebrew Institute of Riverdale and Rabbi Daniel Sperber, Israel. There are close to a thousand women rabbis in the world today.